Close Your Best Sales

Evelyn Wright

Evelyn Wright

Copyright Page

Index

Introduction to Closing Sales

Closing a sale is one of the most important skills a salesperson can develop. No matter how good you are at attracting customers or presenting your product, if you can't close the sale, all your previous efforts will have been in vain. But what does closing a sale actually mean? In simple terms, closing a sale is the moment when the customer decides to buy your product or service. It is the climax of the entire sales process and undoubtedly the most crucial one.

For many salespeople, closing can seem like a daunting task. The anxiety of being rejected or not knowing what to say can be paralyzing. However, closing a sale doesn't have to be a difficult or stressful process. With the right strategies and techniques, you can make closing a natural and effective part of your sales conversation.

First, it's essential to understand the importance of closing the sales. Without an effective close, all your prospecting, presentation, and objection-handling efforts may be in vain. Imagine you've spent weeks cultivating a relationship with a potential customer. You've answered all their questions, resolved all their objections, and clearly demonstrated the value of your product. But in the end, when it comes time to ask for the sale, you're at a loss for words or feel unsure. The customer, sensing your hesitation, decides not to buy. All that investment of time and energy is wasted.

Furthermore, closing the sale is not only crucial to completing the transaction; it is also vital to building long-term relationships with your customers. An effective closing can leave a lasting, positive impression on your customer, increasing the likelihood of future sales and referrals. Conversely, a clumsy or forced closing can damage the relationship and discourage the customer from doing business with you again.

There are different types of sales, and each requires a different closing approach. For example, small sales are typically quicker and less complex. The customer is already predisposed to buying and needs little additional persuasion. In these situations, a straightforward and straightforward close can be very effective. On the other hand, large sales are more complicated and require more time and effort. The customer may need more information, demonstrations, and reassurance before they feel comfortable making a decision. Here, a more strategic and patient approach is crucial.

Closing sales is not just a matter of technique; it is also a matter of mindset. Confidence in yourself and your product is essential. If you do not firmly believe in the value of what you are selling, it will be difficult to convince your customers to buy it. Also, it is important to remember that closing is not a battle against the customer, but a collaboration. Your goal is to help the customer make the best possible decision, which ideally should be the purchase of your product.

An essential part of closing sales is understanding customer psychology. Every customer is different, with their own wants, needs, and fears. Some customers may be very analytical and will need a lot of information and data before making a decision. Others may be more impulsive and make decisions based on emotions or on the recommendation of someone they trust. Identifying and adapting to these different types of customers can make a huge difference in your ability to close sales.

Finally, closing sales is a skill that can be learned and improved with practice. Don't expect to be perfect from the start. Every interaction with a customer is an opportunity to learn and improve. Analyze your closings, both successful and unsuccessful, and look for ways to improve. Over time, you'll become more confident and effective in your ability to close sales.

In short, closing sales is an essential component of the sales process. It's the moment when all your previous work comes together in a transaction. With the right mindset, a deep understanding of your customer, and the right techniques, you can become a master in the art of closing sales. Remember that every customer and every sale is unique, and adaptability is key to success. With practice and dedication, you can develop the skill of closing sales effectively and build lasting relationships with your customers.

Customer Psychology

Understanding customer psychology is essential for any salesperson who wants to be successful. Knowing what motivates a customer, what they care about, and what they really need can make the difference between closing a sale and losing an opportunity. Customer psychology is all about understanding how customers think and behave during the buying process. This knowledge will allow you to tailor your sales approach to better meet their needs and increase your chances of closing the sale.

First, it's important to recognize that every customer is unique. Each person has their own wants, needs, and fears that influence their decision-making process. For example, some customers may be primarily motivated by price and look for the best deal possible. Others may be more interested in product quality or customer service. By identifying these motivations, you can tailor your sales message to address each customer's specific priorities.

To understand customer psychology, it's crucial to develop good listening skills. Actively listening to your customer allows you to gather valuable information about their needs and wants. Pay attention not only to what they say, but also how they say it. Tone of voice, body language, and facial expressions can provide important clues about what they really think and feel. By showing that you're genuinely interested in understanding their needs, you can build a relationship of trust, which is crucial to success in sales.

Another important aspect of customer psychology is the concept of pain points. Pain points are specific problems or challenges that the customer faces that your product or service can solve. Identifying these pain points and offering a clear and effective solution is a powerful way to persuade the customer to make a purchase. For example, if you are selling project management software, a common pain point might be difficulty coordinating work teams. By highlighting how your software can simplify this task and improve efficiency, you can capture the customer's interest and motivate them to buy.

Trust is another crucial factor in customer psychology. Customers prefer to buy from people and companies they trust. To build trust, it's important to be honest and transparent in all your customer interactions. Keep your promises and offer exceptional customer service. You can also use testimonials and success stories from other customers to prove the effectiveness and reliability of your product or service. Trust is built over time, but it's an essential element to consistently closing sales.

Customer decision making is also influenced by their emotions. Emotions play a big role in purchasing behavior, often more than we realize. A customer may make a decision based on how they feel about a product or service, even if it's not the most logical or rational choice. For example, a customer may choose a more expensive car because it makes them feel successful or prestigious. As a salesperson, it's important to connect with the customer's emotions and make them feel good about their purchasing decision. Use stories and examples that resonate emotionally and that showcase the benefits of your product in a way that touches the customer's heart.

In addition to emotions, the perception of value is crucial in customer psychology. Customers want to feel like they are getting a good deal and that the value of what they are buying outweighs the cost. To increase the perception of value, highlight the unique features and benefits of your product. Show how your product can save the customer time, money, or effort, or how it can significantly improve their life. Comparisons with competing products can also help highlight the unique value of your offering.

Risk aversion is another important consideration. Many customers fear making a bad decision and regretting their purchase. To mitigate this fear, offer warranties, flexible return policies, and trial periods. Reassure the customer that if they are not satisfied with their purchase, they will have options to resolve any issues. Reducing the perceived risk can make the customer feel more comfortable and confident in making the purchasing decision.

Finally, it's important to remember that customer psychology isn't an exact science. Every interaction is an opportunity to learn and adjust your approach. Stay alert to customer cues and feedback and use that information to continually improve your sales process. With practice and dedication, you can master the art of understanding customer psychology and use that knowledge to effectively close more sales.

In short, customer psychology is a powerful tool that can help you improve your sales skills. By understanding what motivates your customers, identifying their pain points, building trust, and connecting emotionally with them, you can increase your chances of successfully closing sales. Remember that every customer is unique and that adaptability and empathy are key to understanding and meeting their needs. Over time, this knowledge will allow you to not only close more sales, but also build long-lasting and successful relationships with your customers.

In-Person Closing Strategies

Closing sales in person can be both an exciting and challenging experience. It is in these moments that you have the opportunity to connect directly with your customer, read their non-verbal cues, and adapt your approach in real time. For many salespeople, closing in person is where they can really shine and demonstrate their skills. However, it is also a stage of the sales process that requires preparation, confidence, and a deep understanding of effective closing strategies. In this chapter, we will explore some of the best strategies for effectively closing sales in person.

One of the most fundamental strategies for closing sales in person is the direct close. This approach involves directly asking the customer to make the purchase. It may seem simple, but it is often incredibly effective. Many customers are ready to buy, but they just need a little nudge or a clear signal that it is the right time to do so. For example, after you have presented your product and answered all of the customer's questions, you can say something like, "Would you like to take this product with you today?" or "Can we proceed with the purchase now?" This direct question can help remove any hesitation and move the customer toward the purchasing decision.

Another effective strategy is the alternative close. Instead of asking the customer if they want to buy, you offer them two options to choose from, both leading to a sale. For example, you might say, "Would you prefer the basic model or the advanced model?" or "Would you like to pay with cash or credit card?" By offering options, you reduce the chance of an outright rejection and help the customer feel more in control of the decision. This technique can also be useful in guiding the customer toward an option that offers greater value or benefit.

Scarcity closing is another powerful technique that takes advantage of the customer's fear of missing out on an opportunity. This approach involves highlighting limited product availability or a special, limited-time offer. For example, you could say, "We only have a few units available right now," or "This special offer will only be available until the end of the week." By creating a sense of urgency, you can motivate the customer to make a quick decision and avoid missing out on the purchase opportunity. It's important to be honest and authentic with this strategy so as not to damage customer trust.

The summary closing technique is useful for reinforcing all the benefits and features of the product that you've discussed during the presentation. This approach involves summarizing the key points and then asking for the sale. For example, you could say, "As we've discussed, this product offers you X, Y, and Z benefits. Plus, we have a satisfaction guarantee. Would you like to proceed with the purchase now?" By reminding the customer of all the advantages of the product, you reinforce its value and make the purchase decision clearer and more appealing.

The assumption close is a strategy where you act as if the purchase decision has already been made. This approach can be very effective when you feel that the customer is already convinced but just needs a little final push. For example, you could say, "I'll prepare the purchase documents so you can pick up the product today," or "Let's arrange delivery for next week, is that okay?" By assuming the sale, you demonstrate confidence and can help the customer feel more confident in their decision.

The trial close is a technique that allows the customer to experience the product before making a final decision. This approach can be especially effective for products that require a direct experience to fully appreciate their value. For example, if you're selling a car, you could invite the customer to take a test drive. If you sell exercise equipment, you could offer an in-store demonstration. By allowing the customer to interact with the product, you can remove any hesitation and make them feel more confident in their purchasing decision.

An additional strategy is referral closing, which involves using testimonials and success stories from other customers to persuade the customer to buy. You can share stories of how other customers have benefited from your product and how it has solved similar problems that the current customer is facing. For example, you could say, "A customer similar to yours was facing the same problem and found our product to be the perfect solution.

They have since seen a significant improvement in their efficiency." By providing social proof and concrete examples, you can increase the customer's trust in your product and the purchasing decision.

Finally, it's crucial to remember the importance of empathy and personalization when closing sales in person. Every customer is different, and what works for one may not work for another. Take the time to get to know your customer, understand their needs, and adapt your approach accordingly. Showing empathy and understanding can create a stronger connection and increase the chances of effectively closing the sale.

In short, closing sales in person requires a combination of effective strategies, confidence, and a deep understanding of the customer's needs. From direct and alternative closing to scarcity and trial closing, there are many techniques you can use to guide the customer toward the purchasing decision. The key is to be authentic, empathetic, and adaptable, adjusting your approach to each situation and customer. With practice and dedication, you can master the art of the in-person closing and significantly increase your sales success rates.

Closing Sales by Chat

Closing sales via chat can seem challenging since you don't have the advantage of face-to-face communication. However, with the right strategies, you can turn chat conversations into a powerful sales tool. The key is knowing how to interact effectively, create a connection with the customer, and gently guide them towards the purchasing decision. In this chapter, we'll explore various techniques and tips to effectively close sales via chat.

The first fundamental strategy in closing sales via chat is a quick response. In a world where immediacy is increasingly valued, responding quickly to customer messages can make a huge difference. When a customer contacts you via chat, they are usually looking for quick answers and immediate solutions. By responding promptly, you not only demonstrate professionalism, but you also keep the customer interested, preventing them from looking elsewhere for alternatives.

Another important technique is to personalize the conversation. Customers want to feel like they are talking to a real person and not a bot. Use their name and ask relevant questions about their needs and preferences. For example, if a customer is interested in a specific product, you can ask "What features of this product are most important to you?" or "How do you plan to use this product?" These questions will not only help you better understand the customer's needs, but they will also show that you care about their satisfaction.

It's essential to keep communication clear and concise. In chat, customers don't have the time or patience to read long, complicated messages. Make sure your responses are direct and to the point. Use short, clear sentences to effectively convey your message. If the customer has questions, answer them accurately and offer additional information only when necessary. Clarity in communication can help avoid misunderstandings and keep the customer focused on the buying process.

An effective technique for closing sales via chat is to use soft persuasion. This involves guiding the customer toward the purchasing decision without being pushy or aggressive. For example, after providing the requested information, you can say something like, "Would you like to proceed with the purchase?" or "I can help you finalize your order right now." This subtle suggestion may be all the customer needs to make the purchasing decision. Soft persuasion is especially effective because it creates an environment of cooperation rather than pressure.

Using visuals can also be very helpful in chat. Often, a picture or video can communicate more than words can. If the customer is interested in a specific product, send them high-quality images or videos that show the product in use. These visuals can help the customer visualize the product and better understand its benefits. Additionally, visuals can make the conversation more engaging and keep the customer interested.

Offering exclusive promotions and discounts via chat is another effective strategy. For example, you can say, "Today only, we are offering a 10% discount on this product," or "If you purchase now, you can get free shipping." These exclusive offers can create a sense of urgency and motivate the customer to make a quick decision. Make sure these promotions are clear and easy for the customer to apply.

A crucial aspect of closing sales via chat is following up. Not every customer will be ready to buy right away. Some may need time to think or consult with others. In these cases, it's important to follow up appropriately. You can send a friendly follow-up message, asking if they have any other questions or need more information. For example, "Hi, I just wanted to know if you had a chance to review the information I sent you. Can I help you with anything else?" Following up shows that you care about customer satisfaction and can reignite interest in purchasing.

Additionally, it's important to handle objections effectively. Customers may have questions or concerns about the product or the purchasing process. Instead of viewing these objections as roadblocks, view them as opportunities to clarify and reinforce the value of your product. Listen carefully to the customer's concerns and offer detailed, reassuring responses. For example, if a customer expresses concern about price, you can highlight the additional features and benefits that justify the cost.

Finally, closing sales via chat requires a positive and friendly attitude. The way you communicate can have a huge impact on the customer experience. Make sure you are friendly, patient, and professional at all times. A positive tone can make the customer feel more comfortable and confident in their purchasing decision. Even if the customer doesn't buy right away, a positive interaction can leave a lasting impression and increase the chances of future sales.

In short, closing sales via chat can be a challenging task, but with the right strategies, you can turn every conversation into a sales opportunity. From quick response and personalization to gentle persuasion and the use of visual aids, there are many techniques you can use to guide the customer towards the purchasing decision. Remember to maintain clear communication, offer exclusive promotions, follow up properly, and handle objections skillfully. With practice and dedication, you can master the art of closing sales via chat and significantly increase your sales success rates.

Closing Small Sales

Closing small sales may seem less complicated than closing large sales, but it is still a crucial process that requires its own strategy and approach. Small sales may not generate large revenues per transaction, but they are the lifeblood of many businesses and can often add up to have a significant impact on total sales. Additionally, closing small sales effectively can help build customer relationships and open the door to future, larger sales. In this chapter, we will explore the best strategies for closing small sales effectively and efficiently.

The first key to closing small sales is understanding the value of the product from the customer's perspective. Even though the monetary value may be lower, the product must still fulfill a customer need or desire. It's critical to clearly communicate the benefits of the product and how it can improve the customer's life, even in small ways. For example, if you're selling a cell phone accessory, you can highlight how this accessory will make using the phone more convenient or fun. By focusing the conversation on the benefits, you can help the customer see the value of the product, no matter its price.

Another important strategy is simplicity in the purchasing process. For small sales, the purchasing process should be as simple and straightforward as possible. Customers don't want to spend a lot of time making a decision for a small purchase. Make sure the selection, payment, and delivery process is fast and hassle-free. For example, if you have an online store, optimize the user experience so that they can add products to the cart and complete the purchase in just a few clicks. Simplicity and convenience are essential to successfully closing small sales.

Using special offers and promotions can be very effective in closing small sales. Discounts, buy-one-get-one-free offers, or limited-time promotions can motivate customers to make an immediate purchase. For example, you could offer a 10% discount on purchases under a certain amount or a small gift for every purchase made. These offers can make the product even more attractive and convince the customer that they are getting a good deal. Additionally, promotions can create a sense of urgency, which can speed up the purchasing decision.

Personalization also plays a crucial role in closing small sales. Even though the transaction value may be lower, customers appreciate personalized treatment. Call the customer by name and make recommendations based on their previous purchases or known interests. For example, if a customer has purchased kitchen-related products, you could suggest additional kitchen utensils that complement their previous purchases. Personalization can make the customer feel valued and more likely to complete the purchase.

Product presentation is another important aspect. Even for small sales, the way you present the product can influence the customer's purchasing decision. Make sure products are well presented, with clear descriptions and high-quality photos. If possible, include customer testimonials that highlight the quality and usefulness of the product. Good presentation can make the product look more valuable and attractive, which can help close the sale.

Building trust is essential to closing any sale, including small sales. Make sure the customer feels safe buying your product. Offer satisfaction guarantees or clear return policies so the customer knows they can return the product if it doesn't meet their expectations. Transparency and honesty in communication are also crucial. Answer any questions or concerns the customer may have clearly and honestly. Trust can be a deciding factor in the purchasing decision, even for low-cost products.

Following up is another important strategy for closing small sales. Not every customer will buy on the first contact, and they may need a reminder or a little encouragement to complete the purchase. Send follow-up emails or friendly messages reminding them of the product they were considering. For example, you could send an email saying, "We noticed you were interested in this product. Here's a special discount if you make your purchase today." Following up shows that you value the customer and are willing to help them complete their purchase.

Additionally, offering multiple payment options can make it easier to close small sales. Make sure customers can pay in the way that is most convenient for them, whether it is by credit card, debit card, bank transfers, or mobile payments. The more payment options you offer, the easier it will be for the customer to complete the purchase. Flexibility in payment options can be a deciding factor, especially for low-cost products where the checkout process should not be a hindrance.

Finally, it's important to maintain a positive and enthusiastic attitude throughout the sales process. Customers can sense your energy and attitude, and a positive attitude can make the shopping experience more enjoyable. Even if the sale is small, every interaction with the customer is an opportunity to build a positive relationship that can lead to future sales. Thank the customer for their purchase and let them know you appreciate their business. A positive shopping experience can lead to word-of-mouth recommendations and customer loyalty.

In short, closing small sales requires a combination of understanding the value of the product, simplicity in the purchasing process, special offers, personalization, good presentation, trust building, follow-up, flexible payment options, and a positive attitude. Although each individual sale may be small, the cumulative impact of closing many small sales can be significant for your business. With the right strategies, you can maximize your small sales and build a solid base of satisfied customers.

Closing Large Sales

Closing large sales is an exciting and rewarding challenge in the world of sales. Large sales can have a significant impact on your revenue and business growth. However, they require a different and more detailed strategy than small sales. In this chapter, we will explore various strategies and techniques to close large sales effectively and efficiently.

The first key to closing big sales is research. Before you even contact the client, you need to thoroughly understand their business, their needs, their challenges, and their goals. Do your research on their industry, their market position, and their competitors. The more information you have, the better you can tailor your presentation and proposal to the client's specific needs. Research also allows you to identify the client's pain points and how your product or service can offer a valuable solution.

Once you've done your research, the next step is to establish a strong connection with the customer. Big sales often involve a deeper, longer-lasting relationship with the customer. Take the time to get to know the key people involved in the buying process.

Establishing a relationship of trust is essential. Listen carefully to their needs and concerns, and show a genuine interest in helping them achieve their goals. Trust and credibility are key to closing big sales.

The presentation of your proposal is another crucial aspect. For large sales, the presentation should be detailed and personalized. Make sure your proposal specifically addresses the client's needs and challenges. Use concrete data and examples to back up your claims. For example, if you are selling a technology solution, show how it has helped other similar companies improve their efficiency and reduce costs. A well-structured, fact-based presentation can convince the client that your product or service is the best option.

Product demonstration is a vital part of the closing process for large sales. In many cases, the customer will want to see the product in action before making a decision. Arrange detailed, personalized demonstrations that show how the product can solve the customer's specific problems. Make sure the customer has the opportunity to ask questions and clarify any doubts during the demonstration. A successful demonstration can be the deciding factor that leads the customer to make the purchasing decision.

Handling objections is another important aspect of closing large sales. Customers may have concerns or doubts that need to be addressed before they commit to a major purchase. Listen carefully to the customer's objections and answer them clearly and honestly. Provide evidence and examples to support your answers. For example, if the customer is concerned about cost, you can demonstrate how the return on investment (ROI) justifies the initial expense. Handling objections effectively can help overcome barriers and move you toward closing.

Negotiation is often an unavoidable part of closing large sales. Clients may want to discuss contract terms, price, payment terms, or other aspects of the deal. Be prepared to negotiate in a flexible and professional manner. Establish your boundaries and priorities before the negotiation, but also show a willingness to find a middle ground that satisfies both parties. Successful negotiation involves giving in on some aspects while ensuring that the final agreement is beneficial to your business.

Using testimonials and references is a powerful strategy in closing large sales. Potential clients often look for proof that your product or service has been successful at other similar businesses. Provide testimonials from satisfied customers and references who can speak to their positive experience with your product. Case studies are also useful to show how you have helped other businesses achieve significant results. Social proof can increase client confidence in your proposition.

Ongoing follow-up is essential in the process of closing large sales. Unlike small sales, large sales may require multiple meetings and communications before reaching a final decision. Maintain regular, consistent communication with the client. Send follow-up emails, phone calls, or even in-person visits to maintain interest and address any additional concerns. Following up shows your commitment and can keep the momentum going toward closing.

Offering customized solutions and added value can be a decisive factor in closing large sales. Instead of offering a generic approach, tailor your proposal to align with the client's specific needs and goals. Identify opportunities to add additional value, such as consulting services, extended technical support, or additional training. Showing that you are willing to go above and beyond to ensure the client's success can differentiate you from the competition and strengthen your proposal.

Finally, patience and persistence are essential in closing large sales. These processes can be long and complex, and you may face several obstacles along the way. Maintain a positive and persistent attitude, and do not be discouraged by challenges. Every interaction with the client is an opportunity to move forward and build a stronger relationship. Persistence and dedication can eventually lead you to the successful closing of the sale.

In short, closing big sales requires a combination of thorough research, relationship building, detailed presentations, effective demonstrations, objection handling, flexible negotiation, use of testimonials, ongoing follow-up, customized solutions, and an attitude of patience and persistence. Although the process can be challenging, the rewards of closing a big sale can be significant. With the right strategies and a professional approach, you can increase your chances of success and close big sales that drive growth for your business.

The Power of Persuasion

The power of persuasion is a fundamental tool in the world of sales. The ability to convince someone that your product or service is exactly what they need can make the difference between success and failure in a sale. Persuasion is not about manipulation or deception; it is about effectively communicating the value and benefits of what you offer. In this chapter, we will explore various techniques and strategies to develop and use the power of persuasion effectively and ethically.

To start, it's important to understand that convincing starts with confidence in your own product or service. If you're not completely sure about what you're selling, it's going to be difficult to convince others. Take the time to thoroughly understand your product, its features, benefits, and how it compares to the competition. The more you know, the more convincing you'll be. For example, if you're selling software, you should know its features, the problems it solves, and how it's helped other customers. This confidence will come through in your pitch and allow you to speak with authority and credibility.

Empathy is another powerful tool in convincing. Putting yourself in the customer's shoes and understanding their needs, wants, and concerns will allow you to tailor your message more effectively. Actively listen to what the customer has to say, ask questions to dig deeper into their needs, and show that you truly care about their situation. For example, if a customer is concerned about cost, instead of brushing off that concern, address the issue and explain how the value of the product justifies the investment. Empathy creates an emotional connection and makes the customer feel understood and valued.

Storytelling is an effective technique for persuading. People connect with stories, and a good story can make your product or service more memorable and appealing. Share success stories from other customers who have used your product and seen positive results. For example, if you sell a health product, tell the story of a customer who improved their quality of life thanks to your product. Stories help illustrate the benefits in a tangible way and can make the customer see themselves achieving the same positive results.

Clarity and simplicity in communication are crucial to convincing. Avoid using technical jargon or complicated explanations that can confuse the customer. Instead, use simple, straightforward language that anyone can understand. For example, if you are selling a financial service, instead of using complex terms, clearly explain how the service can help the customer save money or better manage their finances. Simplicity in the message makes it easier to understand and makes it easier for the customer to make an informed decision.

Demonstration is another key technique for convincing. Seeing is believing, and when customers can see the product in action or experience its benefits firsthand, they are more likely to be convinced. Organize demonstrations, free trials, or product samples so customers can try it for themselves. For example, if you sell a beauty product, offer samples so customers can see and feel the results. An effective demonstration can remove doubts and clearly show the value of the product.

Using testimonials and social proof is also very powerful. Potential customers often seek validation from others before making a purchasing decision. Provide testimonials from satisfied customers and success stories that demonstrate the benefits of your product. For example, include customer reviews that highlight how your product has helped them solve a specific problem. Social proof can build trust and make the customer feel more confident in making a decision.

Urgency is a technique that can help speed up the decision process. Creating a sense of urgency can motivate the customer to act immediately rather than putting off the decision. Use limited-time promotions, special discounts, or limited product availability to create this sense of urgency. For example, you could offer a 20% discount that is only available for one week. Urgency can push the customer to take action before they miss out on the opportunity.

Consistency and repetition are essential in the process of convincing customers. Not every customer will make a decision on the first contact. It is important to maintain regular and consistent communication with the customer. Send follow-up emails, offer additional information, and be available to answer any questions or concerns. Repeating the message and continuing contact can keep the customer interested and strengthen your argument.

Authenticity and honesty are key to long-term buy-in. Customers can detect insincerity, and this can erode trust. Be transparent about what your product can and cannot do. If there are limitations, admit them and focus on how you can mitigate those aspects. For example, if you sell software that doesn't have a specific feature that the customer wants, be honest about that, but highlight the other features that may be beneficial. Honesty builds a strong foundation of trust and can make customers respect your integrity.

Finally, practice and continuous learning are key to developing and honing your sales skills. Study communication techniques, take sales courses, and learn from every interaction with clients. Reflect on what worked and what didn't, and adjust your approach accordingly. Continuous improvement will allow you to be more effective in your sales efforts and increase your closing rates.

In short, the power of persuasion in sales is based on a combination of confidence in your product, empathy, storytelling, clarity, demonstration, social proof, urgency, consistency, authenticity, and continuous learning. By applying these strategies ethically and effectively, you can improve your sales skills and increase your chances of success. Persuasion is not about manipulation, but about communicating value clearly and genuinely to help customers make informed and beneficial decisions.

Effective Closing Techniques

Closing a sale is the highlight of any sales process, and to do so effectively, it's crucial to master a variety of closing techniques. Every customer is different, and what works for one may not be effective for another. That's why it's important to have a variety of techniques at your disposal and know when and how to use them. In this chapter, we'll explore some of the most effective closing techniques and how to apply them in a variety of sales situations.

One of the most well-known closing techniques is the direct close. This method involves asking the customer directly and clearly to make a decision. It is a simple but powerful technique. For example, after a thorough presentation of your product, you can ask, "Are you ready to order today?" This type of closing is most effective when you have already built a relationship of trust and the customer has shown interest in your product. The clarity and confidence in your question can motivate the customer to make a quick decision.

Another effective technique is the choice close. Instead of asking if the customer wants to buy, offer them two options to choose from. For example, you could ask, "Do you prefer the standard version or the premium version?" By giving options, the customer focuses on which option to choose rather than whether or not to buy. This technique can be particularly useful for products with different levels of features or services. By offering options, you also demonstrate flexibility and adaptation to the customer's needs.

Closing by assumption is a technique that involves acting as if the purchase decision has already been made. You can begin filling the order or asking specific delivery details as if the customer has already said yes. For example, you might say, "What address would you like us to ship the product to?" This approach can smooth the transition to closing and make the customer feel more committed to the decision. However, it's important to use this technique tactfully so as not to appear presumptuous.

The highlighted benefit closing technique focuses on highlighting a key benefit that is especially important to the customer. During the conversation, you will have identified what matters most to the customer, such as time savings, cost, quality, etc. When closing, emphasize how your product meets that specific need. For example, you could say, "With this product, you can save up to 30% on operating costs." By focusing the closing on a crucial benefit, you can make the purchasing decision more attractive to the customer.

Scarcity closing creates a sense of urgency by indicating that the product or offer is limited. You can mention that there are only a few units left or that the special offer expires soon. For example: "We have only five units left at this special price." This technique can motivate the customer to act quickly so they don't miss out on the opportunity. However, it's important to use scarcity honestly and ethically to avoid damaging customer trust.

The guarantee closing technique offers the customer additional security by providing a guarantee or a return policy. This can reduce the perceived risk for the customer and make them feel more comfortable making the purchase decision. For example, you could say, "If you are not completely satisfied with the product, you have 30 days to return it for a full refund."

The guarantee shows confidence in your product and can be the final push the customer needs to make the decision.

The trial close is a technique where you offer a free trial or a trial period before a full purchase. This allows the customer to experience the benefits of the product without any commitment. For example, you could say, "Try our service for a month at no cost and then decide if you want to continue." This technique can be especially effective for products or services that require a demonstration of their value. The free trial lowers the barrier to entry and can turn the trial into a full sale.

Closing with final questions involves asking a series of questions that lead the customer to make a decision. These questions should be designed to confirm that the customer is ready to buy. For example: "Are you satisfied with the features we discussed?" "Is the price okay with you?" "Do you want to have the product delivered to your home or office?" Each affirmative answer brings the customer closer to closing. This technique can also help you identify and resolve any final objections the customer may have.

Closing by referring to other customers uses social proof to persuade the customer. You can mention how other similar customers have had success with your product or service. For example: "Many of our customers in your industry have seen a significant increase in productivity after using our product." Social proof can reinforce the credibility of your product and make the customer feel more confident in their decision.

Finally, the summary closing technique involves summarizing the key points of the conversation and how your product meets the customer's needs. At the end, you can ask if the customer is ready to proceed. For example: "We've discussed how our product can help you improve efficiency and reduce costs. Are you ready to order?" Summarizing the benefits can reinforce the value of your proposition and help the customer make an informed decision.

In short, mastering a variety of closing techniques can significantly increase your sales success rates. Each technique has its time and place, and the key is knowing when and how to use them. Direct closing, option closing, assumption closing, highlight closing, scarcity closing, guarantee closing, proof closing, closing questions closing, reference to other clients closing, and summary closing are all powerful tools that you can apply in a variety of situations. By understanding and practicing these techniques, you can close sales more effectively and build lasting relationships with your customers. The art of closing sales is a skill that is honed with time and experience, and with the right strategies, you can become a master of closing.

Handling Objections

Objection handling is a crucial skill in the sales process. Objections are a natural part of any sales conversation, and rather than seeing them as an obstacle, you should view them as opportunities to deepen your relationship with the customer and effectively address their concerns. This chapter will explore various strategies and techniques for handling objections so that you can turn those concerns into purchasing decisions.

First, it's critical to understand that objections are not personal rejections, but legitimate concerns that the customer has about the product, price, need, time, or something else. By addressing these concerns with empathy and understanding, you can build a relationship of trust and demonstrate that you truly care about their satisfaction.

One of the most effective techniques for handling objections is active listening. When a customer raises an objection, it's important to give them your full attention and listen without interrupting. Let the customer fully express their concerns before you respond. Not only does this give you a full understanding of the objection, but it also shows the customer that you value their opinion. For example, if a customer says the price is too high, instead of interrupting, let them finish speaking and then address their concern.

Once you've heard the objection, show empathy. Acknowledge the customer's concern and let them know that you understand their point of view. You can say something like, "I understand that the price may seem high, and I appreciate you mentioning that." Empathy helps defuse any tension and makes the customer feel understood.

After demonstrating empathy, it's time to probe deeper into the objection. Ask open-ended questions to better understand the customer's concern. For example, if the objection is about price, you could ask, "Could you tell me more about your concerns regarding price?" This will allow you to gain additional information that can be crucial to effectively addressing the objection. By probing, you also demonstrate that you are interested in finding a suitable solution for the customer.

Once you fully understand the objection, provide an informed response. This response should directly address the customer's concern and offer a solution or insight that may change their mind. For example, if the objection is about price, you could highlight the value and long-term benefits of the product. You could say, "I understand your concern about the initial price, but let me explain how this product can save you money in the long run by reducing operating costs." Provide concrete examples or testimonials from other customers who have found value in the product despite the initial price.

Another useful technique is reframing the objection. This involves changing the customer's perspective on their concern. For example, if a customer objects that they don't have time to learn how to use a new software, you might reframe by saying, "I understand that you're busy, and that's precisely why this software is ideal for you. It's designed to be intuitive and easy to use, which will save you time in the long run." By reframing the objection, you help the customer see the situation from a different perspective that may alleviate their concern.

Sometimes the best way to handle an objection is to anticipate it before it becomes a problem. During your sales presentation, mention common objections other customers have had and how you've addressed them. For example: "Some customers initially have concerns about the price, but once they see the savings and long-term benefits, they find the investment worthwhile." By anticipating objections, you show that you are prepared and have thought about the customer's concerns.

Using social proof can also be effective in handling objections. Mention examples of other customers who had similar concerns and how those concerns were resolved. For example: "One of our customers was also concerned about the price, but after using the product for a few months, they told us that they had recouped their investment thanks to the benefits they gained." Social proof can help build trust and demonstrate that others have found value in your product despite their initial concerns.

In some cases, it can be helpful to offer a guarantee or trial period to alleviate customer concerns. If the objection is about the effectiveness of the product, you might say, "We offer a 30-day money-back guarantee. If you are not completely satisfied, you can return the product at no cost." This offer can reduce the perceived risk and give the customer the confidence to try the product.

It's important to remember that not all objections can be overcome on the spot. If you encounter an objection that you can't resolve right away, be honest and open about it. Say something like, "I understand your concern and want to make sure you get the best response possible. Let me do some more research and I'll get back to you with a solution." This response shows that you value honesty and are committed to finding a suitable solution.

Finally, practice and preparation are key to handling objections effectively. Take time to reflect on common objections you face and develop thoughtful responses to each one. Practice these responses with colleagues or in sales simulations so you feel more confident and prepared when you face real objections.

In short, objection handling is an essential part of the sales process that requires empathy, active listening, research, and informed responses. By addressing customer concerns effectively, you can turn objections into opportunities and build a relationship of trust and respect with the customer. Remember that every objection is an opportunity to demonstrate your knowledge, your commitment, and the quality of your product or service. With the right strategies, you can overcome objections and close more sales effectively.

Post-Closure Follow-up

Post-closing follow-up is an essential part of the sales process that is often overlooked. Once you have closed the sale, you cannot simply call it a day and forget about the customer. Following up is crucial to ensuring that the customer is satisfied, to fostering a long-term relationship, and to opening the door to future sales. This chapter will focus on the importance of post-closing follow-up and best practices for doing it effectively.

After closing a sale, the first step in following up is to thank the customer for their purchase. This simple gesture of gratitude can make a huge difference in how the customer perceives your business. A personalized thank you email, phone call, or even a handwritten note can make the customer feel valued and appreciated. For example, you could send a message saying, "We want to sincerely thank you for your purchase. We are thrilled to have you as a customer and hope you enjoy your product."

The next step in following up is to make sure the customer is happy with their purchase. This involves checking that the product or service meets their expectations and that there are no issues or concerns. You can do this through a follow-up phone call, email, or satisfaction survey. Ask the customer how they are using the product, if they have any questions or problems, and if there is anything else you can do to improve their experience. For example, you could say, "I just wanted to check that everything is okay with your recent purchase. Is there anything I can help you with or any questions you have?"

Following up is also an opportunity to educate the customer on how to get the most value from their purchase. Provide additional tips, tricks, and resources that can help the customer get the most out of the product or service. Not only does this increase customer satisfaction, but it also shows that you care about their success. For example, you could send an email with a link to a tutorial video, a detailed user manual, or a list of frequently asked questions. By providing this information, you are helping the customer feel more comfortable and confident with their purchase.

Another important aspect of post-closing follow-up is asking for feedback. Customer feedback is valuable because it gives you insight into what you're doing well and areas where you can improve. Ask the customer about their experience with the purchasing process, the product or service, and the support they received. Use this feedback to make adjustments and improvements to your business. For example, you could say, "We'd really appreciate your feedback on your recent purchasing experience. Would you please take a few minutes to answer a few questions?"

Following up is also a great opportunity to identify upselling opportunities. During your follow-up interactions, pay attention to the customer's additional needs and wants. You can offer complementary products or services that might interest them. However, it's important to do so in a way that doesn't feel like a hard sell, but rather like a helpful recommendation. For example, you could say, "Based on your recent purchase, we thought you might be interested in this accessory that perfectly complements your product."

In addition to upselling, post-closing follow-up can help foster customer loyalty and build long-term relationships. Maintain regular contact with the customer through newsletters, product updates, and special offers. This ongoing contact helps keep your business top of mind and strengthens the relationship. For example, you could send a monthly email with updates on new products, helpful tips, and exclusive promotions for existing customers.

Another effective strategy in post-closing follow-up is to ask for referrals. Satisfied customers are an excellent source of new leads. Politely ask the customer to recommend your business to friends, family, or colleagues. You can offer incentives such as discounts or rewards for each new referral that turns into a sale. For example, you could say, "If you know someone who could benefit from our products, we would love for you to refer them to us. As a thank you, we will offer a discount on your next purchase for each successful referral."

It's important to remember that post-closing follow-up shouldn't be a one-time task, but rather an ongoing process. Schedule reminders to follow up with customers at different intervals, such as one week, one month, and three months after the purchase. This ensures that the customer feels cared for and valued over time. For example, you could set up a system in your calendar or customer relationship management (CRM) software to remind you to follow up regularly.

In short, post-closing follow-up is a vital part of the sales process that can increase customer satisfaction, foster loyalty, identify upselling opportunities, and gain valuable referrals. By thanking the customer, checking in on their satisfaction, providing additional resources, asking for feedback, identifying upselling opportunities, maintaining regular contact, and asking for referrals, you can build strong, long-lasting relationships with your customers. Remember that every post-closing interaction is an opportunity to demonstrate your commitment to customer success and to strengthen your business in the long run.

In real estate, closing a sale is all about creating an emotional connection with the client. Buying a property is a major decision that is often based on emotional factors as much as practical considerations. To close a sale in real estate, it is critical to highlight the property's unique features and benefits, such as location, layout, amenities, and appreciation potential. Walk-throughs and visual presentations, such as videos and virtual tours, can help clients visualize themselves living in the property. Additionally, it is important to be prepared to negotiate and offer incentives, such as preferential financing or property improvements, to persuade the client to make a decision.

The health and wellness sector presents a different set of challenges and opportunities. Customers in this sector are looking for products and services that can improve their health and quality of life. To close sales in health and wellness, it is essential to establish credibility and trust. This can be achieved by providing scientific evidence, testimonials from satisfied customers, and quality certifications. Empathy and understanding of the customer's individual needs are crucial. For example, in selling nutritional supplements, it is important to explain the specific benefits and how the product can help the customer achieve their health goals. Personalized consultations and health assessments can strengthen the relationship with the customer and make it easier to close the sale.

In the fashion and retail industry, closing sales relies heavily on customer experience. Consumers are looking for products that not only satisfy a practical need, but also offer aesthetic and emotional value. To close sales in this sector, it is important to create a pleasant and engaging shopping experience. Product presentation, store ambiance, and customer service all play a crucial role. Offering special promotions, loyalty programs, and customization options can encourage purchase. Additionally, the use of social media and influencer recommendations can significantly influence customers' purchasing decisions.

The professional services sector, such as consulting and advisory, requires an approach based on relationship building and demonstrating long-term value. Clients in this sector are looking for experts who can offer customized and strategic solutions to their problems. To close sales in professional services, it is important to establish your authority and credibility from the start. Offering free initial consultations, presenting success stories, and providing references from satisfied clients can help gain client trust. Clear and regular communication, along with the ability to demonstrate tangible results, is critical to closing the sale.

The FMCG sector, such as food and beverages, focuses on convenience and perceived value. Customers are looking for products that meet their daily needs quickly and efficiently. To close sales in this sector, it is essential to highlight the quality, competitive price and availability of the product. Promotions, discounts and free samples can encourage purchase. In addition, strategic product placement at key points of sale and effective advertising can increase product visibility and demand.

In the education and training sector, closing the sale involves demonstrating how your product or service can improve the customer's knowledge and skills. Customers in this sector are looking for educational programs that offer high-quality, relevant content. To close sales in education and training, it's important to provide detailed information about the curriculum, the benefits of the program, and the expected outcomes. Offering demonstrations, trial classes, and testimonials from successful students can help persuade customers to enroll. Additionally, it's critical to highlight any accreditations or certifications the program may offer.

Finally, in the entertainment and leisure sector, closing sales is all about creating memorable and exciting experiences. Customers are looking for activities and products that offer them fun and relaxation. To close sales in this sector, it is important to highlight the unique and exciting aspects of the offer. Special promotions, exclusive events and package deals can attract customers. Creative advertising and the use of testimonials from satisfied customers can increase the attractiveness of the offer.

In short, closing sales in different sectors requires an approach tailored to the specific characteristics and needs of each industry. From product demonstrations in technology to creating emotional experiences in real estate to building trust in health and wellness, each sector presents its own challenges and opportunities. By understanding these particularities and applying the right strategies, you can improve your closing skills and increase your success rates in any sector you work in.

Closing Sales in the Digital Environment

In the digital age, closing sales has evolved significantly. Today, many businesses operate online and sales are made through digital platforms. This shift has brought new opportunities and challenges for salespeople. The digital environment offers a wealth of tools and techniques that can help you close sales effectively. In this chapter, we will explore how you can adapt your sales closing strategies to succeed in the digital environment.

First, it's important to understand that in the digital environment, trust and credibility are key. Customers can't see you in person or touch products before purchasing, so they must trust the information you provide them. One way to build trust is to make sure your website or sales platform is professional and easy to navigate. A clean, organized design with clear, detailed product descriptions can make customers feel more comfortable making a purchase.

Another key aspect of closing sales in the digital environment is customer service. In a world where quick responses and personalized service are highly valued, offering real-time support is crucial. Use tools like live chat to answer customer questions immediately. Good customer service can resolve queries and concerns on the spot, which can be decisive in closing a sale. Additionally, ensuring that customers have access to clear information about return and warranty policies can also increase their trust.

Content also plays a crucial role in closing digital sales. Blogs, videos, and product guides can educate customers about the benefits and features of your products. By providing helpful and relevant content, you can influence the customer's purchasing decision. For example, a tutorial video showing how to use a product can help customers visualize how that product fits into their lives, making them more inclined to purchase it. Additionally, testimonials and reviews from other customers can be very persuasive. People tend to trust the experiences of other consumers, so displaying positive testimonials can be an effective strategy to close sales.

Using email marketing is also a powerful strategy in the digital environment. Targeted email campaigns can keep customers interested and engaged. For example, after a customer shows interest in a product, you can send them a follow-up email with more information, special offers, or incentives to complete their purchase. Additionally, emails can be personalized for each customer, increasing the relevance and effectiveness of the message.

Social media is another vital tool for closing sales in the digital environment. Platforms like Facebook, Instagram, and Twitter allow you to interact with customers in a direct and personal way. Posting engaging content and responding to customer comments and questions can help build a closer relationship with them. Additionally, social media allows for highly targeted advertising campaigns, meaning you can target your messages to specific audiences who are more inclined to be interested in your products.

Automation can also be a great ally in the digital environment. Tools like chatbots can provide instant answers to common customer questions, helping to maintain interest and making the purchasing process easier. Additionally, marketing automation systems can send personalized emails and abandoned cart reminders, which can help recover lost sales and close more transactions.

It's important to highlight the importance of user experience in the digital environment. Make sure your online shopping process is as simple and seamless as possible. This includes having a secure and easy-to-use payment system, clear shipping options, and an intuitive interface. The fewer barriers there are in the checkout process, the more likely customers are to complete their purchase.

Data analysis is also a valuable tool in the digital environment. Use analytics tools to understand your customers' behavior online. This can give you insights into which products are most popular, which pages receive the most visits, and at what point customers tend to abandon their shopping carts. With this information, you can make strategic adjustments to improve your conversion rate and close more sales.

Promotions and special offers are another effective tactic in the digital environment. Limited-time discounts, flash sales, and exclusive discount codes can create a sense of urgency that motivates customers to purchase. Additionally, free shipping offers or "buy one, get one" promotions can be attractive incentives for online customers.

Finally, personalization is key in the digital environment. Customers value personalized experiences that fit their preferences and needs. Use customer data to personalize their shopping experiences, from product recommendations to the emails they receive. The more relevant the shopping experience is to the customer, the more likely they are to complete a purchase.

In short, closing sales in the digital environment requires a multifaceted approach that combines trust, customer service, relevant content, email marketing, social media, automation, user experience, data analytics, promotions, and personalization. By applying these strategies, you can adapt to the particularities of the digital environment and maximize your chances of effectively closing sales. The key is to keep the customer at the center of all your actions, providing a positive and satisfying shopping experience that encourages loyalty and future purchases.

Developing Closing Skills

Developing effective closing skills is essential for any salesperson who wants to succeed in their career. Closing the sale is the highlight of the entire sales process, and mastering this skill can make the difference between a successful sale and a missed opportunity. In this chapter, we will explore various strategies and techniques that will help you improve your closing skills and become a more effective and persuasive salesperson.

First, it is crucial to understand that closing a sale is not a one-off event, but rather the result of a series of well-managed interactions with the customer. From the first contact to the completion of the sale, each step must be carefully planned and executed. This means that you must be a good listener, identify the customer's needs, and adapt your approach to meet those needs. Developing this active listening ability is crucial to truly understanding what the customer is looking for and how you can offer them an appropriate solution.

One of the most important techniques for developing closing skills is to practice the art of asking effective questions.

Open-ended questions, which invite the customer to share more information about their needs and wants, are especially helpful. For example, instead of asking, "Do you like this product?" you could ask, "How do you think this product could help you in your day-to-day life?" Not only do these types of questions provide you with more valuable information, they also show the customer that you are genuinely interested in understanding their situation and offering a personalized solution.

Empathy is another key skill in closing sales. Putting yourself in the customer's shoes and seeing things from their perspective will allow you to better connect with them and gain their trust. When a customer feels that you understand them and care about their needs, they are more likely to feel comfortable making the purchasing decision. Empathy also helps you handle objections more effectively, as you can address the customer's concerns with understanding and offer solutions that truly address their concerns.

Preparation is key to a successful sales close. Before every interaction with a customer, make sure you are well prepared.

This includes thoroughly knowing your product or service, understanding the customer's needs and wants, and anticipating potential objections. Preparation gives you the confidence to handle any situation that may arise during the closing process. Plus, it allows you to personalize your approach and present your offer in a way that resonates most with the customer.

The trial closing technique is a useful tool to gauge the customer's interest and willingness before making the final close. For example, you can ask, "How would you feel if you could start using this product today?" or "Do you see any obstacles to moving forward with this purchase?" These questions allow you to gauge the customer's state of mind and adjust your approach as needed. If the customer is hesitant, you can address their concerns before attempting to close the sale.

Clear and concise communication is essential when closing sales. Make sure your message is easy to understand and avoid using technical jargon that can confuse the customer. Use simple, direct language to explain the benefits of your product or service and how it can meet the customer's needs. Additionally, it's important to be transparent and honest in your communications. Customers appreciate sincerity and are more willing to trust you if they feel you're being genuine.

Regular practice is crucial to developing and honing your closing skills. Like any other skill, sales closing improves with consistent practice. Participate in sales simulations with colleagues, look for opportunities to sell in different contexts, and reflect on your experiences to identify areas for improvement. Feedback from your colleagues or supervisors can also be invaluable in helping you refine your approach and develop new strategies.

Another effective technique is the use of testimonials and success stories. Sharing stories from other satisfied customers who have used your product or service can be very persuasive. Testimonials provide social proof that can help convince the customer that they are making the right decision. Additionally, success stories can concretely show how your product or service has helped others in similar situations, which can increase the customer's confidence in their purchasing decision.

Finally, perseverance is an indispensable quality for any salesperson. Not every sale will close on the first try, and it is important not to be discouraged by rejection or objections. Instead of seeing it as a failure, view each interaction as an opportunity to learn and improve. Maintain a positive attitude and continue to look for ways to offer value to the customer. Perseverance, combined with an attitude of continuous improvement, will help you become a more effective and successful sales closer.

In conclusion, developing closing skills requires a combination of active listening, empathy, preparation, clear communication, regular practice, use of testimonials, and perseverance. By working on these areas and applying them consistently in your sales interactions, you can increase your closing rates and become a more effective and persuasive salesperson. Remember that closing sales is both a science and an art, and that success comes with constant practice and dedication.

Conclusion and Final Thoughts

Getting to the end of this book on closing sales is just the beginning of your journey toward becoming a master in the art of closing deals. Throughout the chapters, we've explored numerous strategies, techniques, and skills that are essential to achieving successful closings. Now, it's time to reflect on what you've learned and consider how you can apply this knowledge in your daily professional life.

Closing sales is more than just a transaction; it's a skill that requires empathy, patience, and a deep understanding of the customer's needs. Every customer is unique, and every sale presents its own challenges and opportunities. That's why it's crucial to approach every interaction with an open mind and a genuine desire to help the customer find the solution that best fits their needs.

One of the most important lessons is the importance of preparation. Being well prepared for each sales interaction gives you the confidence to handle any situation that may arise. Knowing your product or service thoroughly, anticipating potential objections, and having a clear plan for each stage of the sales process will allow you to present yourself as a confident and trustworthy professional.

Another key to successful sales closing is the ability to actively listen. Listening attentively to your customers not only allows you to better understand their needs and wants, but it also shows them that you value their perspective. When customers feel that you hear and understand them, they are more likely to trust you and be willing to move forward with a purchase.

Empathy plays a crucial role in closing sales. Putting yourself in the customer's shoes and seeing things from their perspective allows you to connect with them on a deeper level. Empathy not only helps you gain the customer's trust, but it also allows you to handle objections more effectively as you can address their concerns with understanding and offer solutions that truly solve their problems.

Clear and concise communication is essential at every stage of the sales process, but especially at the close. Explaining the benefits of your product or service in a simple and direct way helps the customer see the value you are offering. Avoiding technical jargon and being transparent in your communications builds trust and makes it easier for the customer to make decisions.

Constant practice and perseverance are key to developing and honing your closing skills. Participating in sales simulations, looking for opportunities to sell in different contexts, and reflecting on your experiences will allow you to identify areas for improvement and develop new strategies. Don't be discouraged by rejection or objections; instead, see them as opportunities to learn and grow.

Using testimonials and success stories can also be a powerful tool in closing sales. Sharing stories from satisfied customers who have used your product or service provides social proof that can help convince the customer that they are making the right decision. These testimonials and success stories concretely show how your product or service has benefited others, which can increase the customer's confidence in their purchasing decision.

Finally, it's important to remember that closing sales is both a science and an art. It requires a combination of proven techniques and interpersonal skills that are developed over time. Maintain an attitude of continuous improvement and always look for new ways to offer value to your clients. Dedication and consistent effort will lead you to become a more effective and successful sales closer.

In conclusion, mastering the art of sales closing takes practice, perseverance, and a true dedication to understanding and meeting customer needs. By applying the strategies and techniques discussed in this book, you can improve your closing skills and increase your success rates. Remember that every interaction with a customer is an opportunity to learn and grow. Keep a positive attitude, keep honing your skills, and above all, never stop looking for ways to improve and provide better service to your customers. With time and dedication, you will become a master in the art of sales closing, able to close any deal with confidence and success.

www.ingramcontent.com/pod-product-compliance
Lightning Source LLC
Chambersburg PA
CBHW031124160726
47989CB00016B/1144